ROOMRIMES

ROOMRIMES

POEMS BY SYLVIA CASSEDY

ILLUSTRATIONS BY MICHELE CHESSARE

THOMAS Y. CROWELL   NEW YORK

Library of Congress Cataloging-in-Publication Data
Cassedy, Sylvia.
    Roomrimes.

    Summary: Twenty-six alphabetically arranged poems,
each describing a room or a place ranging from
"Attic" to "Zoo."
    1. Children's poetry, American.   [1. American
poetry]   I. Chessare, Michele, ill.   II. Title.
PS3553.A7953R6 1987   811'.54   86-4583
ISBN 0-690-04466-6
ISBN 0-690-04467-4 (lib. bdg.)

In memory of Nana

CONTENTS

ATTIC

Along the wall
the shadows stand
like flowers pressed
against a page;
each holds a slender
spider strand
and weaves
a monkey-puzzle cage,
entangling
in its silver strings
a company of silent things:

A crowd of husks
where wasps once hummed;
a shrouded couch
with silenced springs;
a mandolin, unstrung,
unstrummed;

1

a tray of butterflies
whose wings
have lost
their fragile
whisperings;
a dinner bell
with silent tongue;
a golden hunting horn
whose note
has withered
in its hollow throat;
a cuckoo bird,
its word unsprung.

If I should tear
this filigree—
if with a finger
I should slash
this web,
this sticky snare—

would I set free
a sudden raucousness
of song,
a symphony
perhaps
of whisper
murmur
jingle
crash
and bong?

BASEMENT

In the damp,
in the cold,
in the basement dark—
so soundlessly
no one would know—
things grow.
Mold, for one.
An arc of mold,
soft as the fluff
in the crease
of a cuff
and smelling
divinely
of rot,
steadily spreads,
steadily coats
a clot
of golden onionheads,
fuzzing their scalps,
bearding their throats.

And buds.
In the still,
in the chill,
in the basement night,
buds grow.
Here in the bin:
rubbery buds—
purple, pale rose,
soap suds white,
and stiff as claws
of new-hatched chicks—
sprout from the dust
of potato pocks,
stretch, thrust,
tickle, scratch,
break the skin
of burlap sacks,
set out alone
on secret tracks.

And something besides:
A squiggle of bugs—
so tiny at first
ten thousand could nap
in a soda-pop cap—
secretly wriggles,
wiggles its toes;
day by day,
hour by hour,
grows;
soon shreds
the threads
of its silk cocoon;
tugs, jerks,
bursts in a shower
of silver-gray sparks,
filling the dark
with a sudden,
a silent,
an instant display
of winged fireworks.

Slime grows, too,
and scale.
Lime-green slime
that climbs on walls
and crawls on floors;
and kale-green scale
in which,
with just a fingernail,
I trace,
where no one else can see,
a face,
an alphabet,
a tale enclosed
within a heart: HE
LOVES ME.
Slime and scale,
in the wet,
in the chill,
in the basement dark—
they grow.

CLOSET

Just what *is* it
in the closet
that I positively
hear?

       Does it
guzzle? is it
grizzled? does it
dazzle? is it
frazzled? has it
nozzles? was it
muzzled? does it
nuzzle in your ear?

If I razz it
or displease it,
if I tease it
or surprise it,
if I faze it
or amaze it,
will I cause it
to appear?

If the whoozit
in the closet
should inquisitively
visit—
just *suppose* it
pays a visit—
should I praise it
or confuse it?
should I daze it
or amuse it?
will I lose it
if I seize it?
will I bruise it
if I squeeze it?
will I freeze it
if I hose it?
will I please it
or abuse it
if I use it
as a spear?

Just what is it
that is nearly,
just what is it
that is clearly,
just what is it
in the closet
that is positively
here?

DEN

And now the den—a warm retreat
with things on which to rest one's feet:
for him, a cushioned ottoman;
for her, an ottowoman;
a place to lounge in easy chairs,
with blankets tucked around one's knees,
and idly study world affairs
in magazines and quarterlies.
Or, bored with that, one simply might
sedately cleanse a reading glass,
and, through its lens, examine things:
an insect bite, a blade of grass,
a heap of silver termite wings.

Lions often live in dens.

ELEVATOR

DOWN

One wall
a door,
the
others
bare;
no
win-
dow,
table,
pic-
ture,
chair;
a gloom-
y,
tomb-
like
room,
and
small—
no
larger
than
a
show-
er
stall.

more.
or
away
feet
ty
nine-
later
ment
mo-
a
just
exit
and
door
gle
sin-
its
through
Enter
vator.
ele-
the
room
a
odd
How

UP

FIRE ESCAPE

Fire-escape time:
8 PM, mid-July,
90 degrees.
Slowly I climb
across a row
of flowerpots,
squeeze past mops
propped in pails
like lollipops,
and perch upon
my iron porch—
that bracket
stuck to brickwork
like a buckle
on a boot—
perch upon
the fire escape,
and wait....

Soon the sun,
a fat balloon
of poppy red,
will slip between
the two tall walls
across the street,
scrape its head
on either side,
coast, glide,
float, slide,
and set
each windowpane
aflame.
Floor by floor—
11,
10,
9,
mine.

It rests its chin
now on the rail,

grins its frail,
its fragile, grin,
and then begins
its slow descent
to jail:
One moment,
two, three,
four,
and then,
and then,
it's mine, *mine!*
Locked, caged,
a raging bull
with blazing eye,
it beats its head
against the bars
while I,
I crouch against
the windowsill
and taunt it
with a swinging key.

Mine, *mine!*

Until I choose
to set it free,
set its bloated
face afloat,
down,
down,
from floor
to floor—
7,
6,
5,
4,
down,
down,
until it splashes
on the ground,
and streaking
through
a stricken sky,
its golden
fire escapes.

GREENHOUSE

In wintertime,
thick flakes sticking to my cheek like licked stamps,
I tramp across the grass
to the greenhouse.

The greenhouse—
that bottle of summer afloat in the snow,
where squads of mottled palm trees grow
and pods like turkey wattles hang—fat, full,
wet with sweat.

The greenhouse!
That's where I go, that's where I stand,
while out in the dark—so cold, so cold—blizzards blow
and scraps of snow die at the walls like froth-winged moths
sizzling in the spark
of a bug trap.

The greenhouse!
That's where I wait, straight and stiff, as if some hand,
some giant hand, might grasp that crooked globe of glass,
and, giving it a sudden shake, let fall another blizzard still:
soft...serene...a silent storm
of green.

HAUNTED ROOM

To and fro,
to and fro:
What makes the empty rocker go?
What makes the window curtain blow?
Someone, someone
lives here. Who?
Some *two*, perhaps.
Some finger taps a midnight waltz
along the piano keys and snaps
the photo album shut.
Some hand unseen advances, halts,
and all at once the window blind
turns somersaults around its pole,
a shiver
stirs the fern's green spine,
and in a bowl the columbine
uplifts its gold-combed head
and quivers in the sudden cold.

To and fro,
to and fro:
Across the wall the cobwebs blow.
A silent hand upsets a row
of soldiers, stiff as dominoes,
and throws a mug of ginger ale
across the rug. A fingernail
inscribes a name—all curlicues
like spider trails—above the door,
while on the floor a pair of shoes
meanders slowly to and fro.
To and fro,
to and fro:
Across the floor the footsteps go.
WHOSE?

IMAGINARY ROOM

To fashion a room—
a room of your own—
fasten your hands
one to the other,
hollow to hollow,
as though
you were holding
a bird—
a swallow, let's say,
or a finch:
something small,
pinched,
and pressed
in the well
of your palms
like an almond
at rest
in its shell.

Now:
Slowly, slowly,
parting your thumbs
no more than an inch,
let him go.
Don't follow his flight;
it's the space
left behind
that we want:
that chamber of night—
dark, round—
with pink threads of light
where your fingers
make chinks.

Hold it up to your eye
and look in.
In the moment or two
it would take you to spin
a binocular wheel,
it will come into view—
There!
It's a *room*:
A tiny bright room
with windows and doors,
a ceiling and floor,
and a circular stair;
a room of your own
where nobody goes,
that nobody knows,
that nobody sees
but you.

Equip it
however you please.

JUNGLE GYM

A giant
once
in idle play
shook out
his box
of pick-up-sticks,
arranged them
neatly,
this way,
that:
a stack
of geometric tricks—
rhombus,
oblong,
square,
trapeze,
perpendicularities;
quadrant,
cuboid,
hexagon,
parallelepipedon.

"How nice,"
he said
when he
had done.
"But uses
it has
plainly
none."

KEEP

The keep is where the keys are kept,
the ring, the crown, the ruby comb;
where heaps of diamond dust are swept
by one whose castle is his home.

LOFT

The loft—
a place for hidden things:

Beneath a clump of tumbleweed,
   four naked mice—little,
   pink,
   wrinkled,
   brittle-kneed;
   fists soft as thistle fuzz,
   eyes sealed tight
   as pumpkin seeds; each
   belly more small
   than the ball
   of a thumb—
   slippery,
   humped,
   plump,
   crumpled as a parboiled peach.

High in the dark of a beam,
   a fat-throat bat—
   hung like a coat
   with ragged sleeves,
   black as leaves
   molding on the floor
   of a stream.

Snug in a nest
   of timothy dust
   and masked in hay,
   a dusk-gray cat—
   flat as a scatter rug,
   stiff of whisker,
   brisk of claw,
   its waking eye
   a frost-green marble
   tossed by some
   forgotten thumb
   and gone astray.

Deep, deep in a crush of hay,
   still as a heap
   of tangled wash,
   knees angled in twisted V's,
   fingers mingled
   fist to fist—
   my sister,
   fast asleep,
   and me.

MIRROR

I wonder this:
The silent boy
without a name
who lives
inside the mirror frame—
does he have dreams?
and do his dreams,
just like his toys,
match mine?
When silently
he screams at night,
his knees drawn
tight in pyramids,
his fingers white
as codfish skin,
what has he seen?
What beast has smashed
the black-green dark
behind his lids?
The wolf?

The slash-jawed wolf
with tattered claw
and crooked grin
whose twin
has wakened *me*?

And something more:
Where does he go,
that nameless boy?
Where does he go
each morning when
he shuts his door?
Is there perhaps
some other stair,
some double of
my door below,
some other street,
some other garden,
maybe,
where,

swinging from some
other tree,
he wonders
what's become of
me?

NEST

Upon my bedroom windowsill
there sits a smaller bedroom still.
The bed is built of dogwood twigs
and lined with dandelion floss;
its spread is made of tansy sprigs,
its quilt of woven willow wands,
its pillowcase of bronze-green moss
arrayed with bands of Queen Anne's lace.

Behind the leafy window shade
a row of feathered heads is laid:
five disheveled babes—no, *six*—
all nestled in a bed of sticks.
Each day they're fed their tea in bed—
alfalfa seed and graham bread—
and when they've settled down to sleep,
their mama cautions, "Not a peep!"

OFFICE

It lacks
a plaque upon the door;
it lacks, in fact,
a door; but otherwise,
it's all equipped:
The walls
are crisscrossed
willow strips;
the chair, a rounded
mound of moss;
the desk, a cube
of stone; the phone,
a clover wired
to the ground.
The sun sends down
a tube of light
and now and then
a circling blade
of wicker
stirs the air.

There's work to do:
Mail comes, for one.
Through slatted slots
along the wall,
frail letters fall: Pale
green and speckled tan,
deckle-edged and scrawled
in fragile manuscript,
they're all
addressed to me. Lapped
across my knee,
they make a fan; piled
behind the tree,
a secret file.

And guests call....
Week after week
on small sharp feet
they pick their way
across the floor—

in furs,
in plumes,
in sleek
red vests,
or trailing veils
of silken thread,
they speak
their coded
messages.

Here.
In this room,
in this room
by the tree,
in this moss-
frosted room
where I stay,

where I'm boss.

PARLOR

Prim and proper
Is the parlor.
Slop not,
Flop not,
In the parlor.
Be not
Snarler,
Gnarler,
Quarreler.
Hop not,
Skip not,
Drop not,
Trip not,
Slap not,
Clap not,
Rip not,
Drip not.

Trim and prim be
In the parlor.
Dumb and glum be,
Dim and grim be,
Numb and mum be,
Namby-pamby,
Prim and proper
In the parlor.

QUIET ROOM

Hush!
This is the quiet room.
Quiet and soft
as an overstuffed lap,
the throat of a thrush,
a cushion of plush,
the whiskery tuft
of a mushroom cap,
marshmallow soft.
Quiet as the fall
of a flake of snow
on the black-ice crust
of a lake;
quiet as a ball
of dust let go
by the shake of a mop;
quiet as the drop
of an ash.

Hush!
This is the quiet room,
where ladybugs
and spiders step
through woolly rugs
on cautious toes,
and close their lips
with fingertips
slim as strands of silk;
where mittened cats
and slippered kittens,
shawled in furs
from tail to cheek,
hold whispered chats
in muffled squeaks
and stifled purrs,
and speak of silent haunts
where shutters never creak
nor shadows stir.
Hush!

ROOF

Here's what to do
on the roof:
First,
with the flick
of a stick,
burst
all the clusters
of blisters
of tar;
let their
licorice ooze
spurt
through the holes
in the soles
of your shoes.

Then,
with a shake
of your hand,
let a pennant
of pigeons,

banded in purple
and lavender-gray,
unfurl in the sky,
swirl low,
high,
uncurl its tail,
sail away.

Now,
with the rim
of a spoon,
hammer the chimney pots—
char-black as swallows,
hollow as bottles—
chime a tune,
a psalm,
a chimney-pipe hymn:
somber,
calm,
brimful of boom.

Last,
stand still.
Stand totally still
in this vastest of rooms,
while chill,
tattered chips
peel
from its ceiling,
drip,
slip,
scatter among
tar bursts
and pigeon nests,
finally
coming to rest
on your nose,
your wrists,
your outstretched tongue.

SHELL

The shell
is parlor to the clam.
It lies,
unlike most living rooms,
beside the booming seas,
where skulls of blackfish
wash ashore;
where schooners sank
and spilled their store
of golden beads
among the frilled anemones;
where sirens sing
amid the reeds
and mermaids swim.

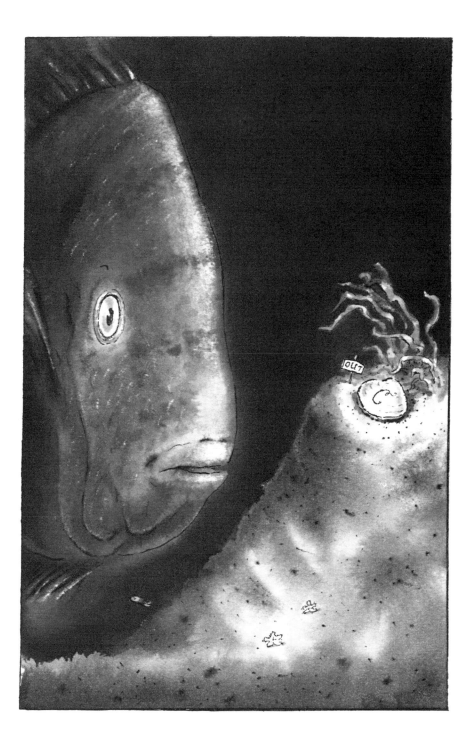

The shell
is parlor to the clam.
Its door,
embellished with
a monogram of C's
(for Clam),
is open just a crack
to let the breezes in,
and there,
upon a pillow sham
of polished, white shellac,
the clam relaxes on his back,
a seaweed ribbon at his chin.

The shell
is parlor to the clam,
and should you lay
a finger
on the lacy fringe
of foam
along its floor
and say,
"Are you at home?"
the door
would slam
upon its single hinge,
and from within,
in what a clam
believes to be a shout,
he'd say, "I am,
it just so happens,
OUT!"

TUNNEL

Tunnel in the park:
a sandwich of night between
two slices of light.

UPSTAIRS

Upstairs
is where the bathroom is.
Upstairs
is where the doorbell rings.
Upstairs
is where you left your pen,
your ballet shoes,
your cowboy things,
the Ping-Pong ball,
the scissors,
when
    you're
        playing
           in
              the
                basement.

VESTIBULE

Apartment houses, as a rule,
are entered through a vestibule,
where anyone who pays a visit
must choose an answer for "Who is it?"

"It is I" (not "me") will do
if there should be just one of you....

But should you be more numerous,
then "It is we" is right (not "us").

WIDOW'S WALK

High, high up
on the widow's walk,
a spyglass fixed
against her eye,
she stands
and scans the skin
of the sea.
Day after day,
until, some say,
the tip of a mast,
slim as a spear
of meadow grass,
will appear at last
at the ocean's brim,
like the thread-thin
hair of a fly
reaching the rim
of a cup.

X

Next
to the room
with window X'd,
the black-shawled crow
clings
to the bricks
with chalk-stained claws.
"Your go,"
he sings
to his
waxed-winged mate.
"Your go,"
he caws;
pauses,
withdraws,
waits
for her
to play the O.

YOUR ROOM

Your room is a mess:

Driftings of dust
are all
clustered beside
the posts
of your bed
like the ghosts
of old mice,
and no one
would guess
that the thing
on your chair
is the dress
that you wear
when you try
to look nice.

There's no place to sit:

Smack in the pit
of your bed
is a sack
of what looks
to be spiders
or whacking-
big fleas,
and the floor
is all spread
with a layer
of grit
that makes pocks
in my socks
and the backs
of my knees.

Your stuff is a wreck:

Your bear
has no hair
on the scruff
of his neck,
the brass
on your trumpet
has lost
all its shine,
your records
have scratches,
your crayons
have specks,
and the door latch
attaches
with snatches
of twine.

(So why,
if your room
is distinctly
a sty,
does it seem
so decidedly
nicer than
mine?)

ZOO

For comfort and pleasure
where troubles are few
there's nothing to rival
a room at the zoo—
with breakfast for two,
a morning shampoo,
and nothing to do
the afternoon through
but sit by the window
and gaze at a view
of caribou,
kinkajou,
shrew,
gnu,
and you.